THE
FATHER'S HEART

MARY NGANGA

TABLE OF CONTENTS

WALK WITH HIM 5

THE WORK OF THE HOLY SPIRIT 17

WHAT IS OUR DESTINY? 22

HOW CAN WE WALK WITH GOD? 28

WHAT DOES IT TAKE TO WALK WITH GOD? 36

HOW CAN WE OVERCOME DISTRACTIONS? 44

WHAT IS THE OUTCOME? 54

BENEFIT OF WALKING WITH GOD 61

ACKNOWLEDGEMENT

Special thanks to Lee Conway, who had given me advice and confirmation that I can produce a material which is readable, advisable and teachable. He has introduced me to people who took me to the next level. Special thanks to Dr.Vincent Gibogwe, who has also took me from one level to the next, proofreading assisting, advising and directing. Special thanks to Bishop Steve Kasuvu who assisted in giving me connections and support in every step that I needed. He made sure the book is completed and is beneficial to readers. Special thanks to John from White Fox who assisted me in different ways. I thank Proerica and Waqar Nadeem from Fiverr for their beautiful work. I appreciate you, may God bless you in abundance. I also thank everyone who prayed for me, encouraged me, and assisted me in one way or the other, everyone who told me "you can do it", I appreciate you all. May God remember you, and bless you.

WALK WITH HIM

Our Father's desire is to fellowship with man which was even before the creation. I can imagine the Father having a meeting, in Genesis 1:26, between Son and the Holy spirit, may be the whole of the Kingdom of Heaven. Saying let us make mankind into our own image, after our likeness, and let them have complete authority over the fish, the sea, the birds of the air, the beast, and over everything that creeps upon the earth. God breathed on the man and there was life and that is why the man is totally incomplete without God, he is always running to seek satisfaction which can only be found when he connects himself with the masterpiece. A man is like a puzzle that is incomplete without God. Sometimes man not satisfied or happy because of what is happening around him, for example, poverty, relationship, family, race, war, misunderstanding and appearance. All these are shadows, the solution is God, for He is the answer. With Him there is harmony, there is love for self, and love for the community as well. But all what we need is to connect with God. Sometimes we are like children who think they know everything, but they come to realise when it is too late, that their parent's advice was the best.

The man had been trying to connect with God but the flesh has been weak, therefore, God brought His only begotten Son whom after His death on the cross promised to bring a helper in, John: 14:26, '' the comforter, counsellor, helper, intercessor, encourager, the Holy Spirit, whom the father will send in my name to represent me and act on my behalf, who will teach you all things. And He will cause you to recall or remember everything I have told you.'' So, all what the man need is to take time in prayers, with a lot of patience, seeking God's guidance, slowing our pace to walk in His pace, especially when prayers delay, God's timing is always the best. The Holy Spirit will guide us if we allow Him, let Him have his way, put your hands in his hand and let him lead. Look up high and see the Lord, He will clear the way for you. God has given us a choice, choose to imitate Him and to glorify Him in every way.

In Colossians1:10-23 NIV, Paul is praying for us to live a life worthy of the Lord and that we may please Him in every way, bearing fruits in every good work, growing in His knowledge, being strengthened with all power according to His glorious might, so that we may have great endurance, patience, and joyfully giving thanks to the Father, who has qualified us to share in the inheritance of the saint in the kingdom of light. For He has rescued us from the dominion of darkness and brought us into the kingdom of the son whom He loves, in whom we have redemption, the forgiveness of our sins. Who is the image of the invisible God, the first-born over-all creation? For by Him all things were created, things in Heaven, earth, visible and invisible, whether thrones or powers or rulers or authorities, all things were created by Him and for Him. He was before all things, and in Him all things hold together. And He is the head of the body, the church, He is the beginning and the firstborn from among the dead, so that in everything He might have the supremacy. For God was pleased to have all His fullness dwell in Him, and through Him to reconcile to Himself all things, whether things on earth or in heaven, by making peace through His blood, shed on the cross. Once we were separated from God and were enemies in our minds because of our evil behaviour. But now He has reconciled us with Christ's physical body through death to present us holy in His sight, without blemish and free from accusation. If we continue in faith, established and firm, not moved from hope held out in the gospel. This is the gospel that has been proclaimed to every creature under the heaven and of which we are all servants.

Sin separated man from God, the beauty of creation became fear between them. The darkness became the talk of the day. The man had to hide from a true friend and a father whom they had been walking for years together, discussing, and making new decision of what should be done or added to what they already had. Genesis 3:8, tells us that, Adam and Eve heard God walking in the garden in the cool of the day, but they hid themselves from the presence of God among the trees of the garden. When sin crawls in our life there is fear and we start seeing things in our evil mind. You can see Adam and eve here before they never knew that they were naked, but after the fall they could not face God, for they realised that they were naked. The lord called Adam and said to him, where are you? He said, ''I heard the sound of you walking in the garden, and I was afraid because I was naked, and I hid myself.'' And the Lord God asked, who told you that you were naked? Have you eaten the tree I commanded you not to eat? And the man was separated from the gift of walking with God to a curse of toiling the earth.

But after this dead rock, we see a man who made a choice to walk with God even after the fall whom God accepted as righteous. We see him in Genesis 5:22-24, his name was Enoch, who lived in a time that man had lost hope of being connected with God. By this time Cain had killed his brother for God favouring his offering. Abel had a heart to please God, but his brother was not. Enoch walked with God for 300 years, until he could not taste death because he was taken by God, for he was pleasing to Him. And because of walking with God, his spiritual eyes were opened to see the lords coming, thousands of years after his time. This is one of the benefits of walking with God, you can see things before they happen. Jude 14-16, emphasis that Enoch prophesied about the world today, he saw the Lord coming with many thousands of his lovely ones, to execute judgement upon all, and to convict all the ungodly, of all their ungodly deeds, which they have done in ungodly way, and of all the harsh things which ungodly sinners have spoken against God. These are complainers, fault seekers, following their own lusts, speaking arrogantly, pleasing people for the sake of gaining an advantage. Enoch is one of the most difficulty to understand, he was mysterious, but he walked with God.

However, even today, if we seek God, we can find Him, the bible tells us to seek and we will find, knock and the door will be opened for us, ask and it shall be given to us and I am at the door knocking, whoever will open I will enter and eat with him. For everyone who ask, receive, and he who seek, finds, and to him who knocks, the door shall be opened. After the fall of man, Enoch found Him, he recovered the most basic call of man, which had been lost, the relationship which the man has been called to have with God, and therefore, Enoch was delivered from the consequence of the fall, which is death. Walking with God remain the final and the highest quest of man. When we truly recover these searches, we too will be delivered from the consequences of the fall of man. 1 Corinthians 15: 51-52, says that, we will not sleep, we shall all be changed in a moment, like in a twinkling of an eye, at the last trumpet, for the trumpet will sound and the dead will be changed. Enoch was the first fruits of the last day church that will also be caught up without tasting death.

If we walk with God, he will bring us into the fullness of His presence, transforming us from mortal to immortal. For us to be where He is desiring, we need to know His moral principles. John 3:30, says that, He must increase but we must decrease. If we try to decrease before He increases in our lives, we will be empty, and the void will be filled with an evil religious spirit. If we walk with God, we decrease because, He is increasing in our life. The reason why our lord and saviour Jesus came, is to make our life better and easier. He also came to change us by destroying the flesh in us, which help us to remove the sin that entangle around us. Even though Enoch did not taste death in the natural, his old nature was consumed by Gods presence. He was not because by walking with God, His glory changed him, consuming his fallen nature, and replacing it with His nature. What is our aim or goal today? Is it possible to imitate Enoch, to die in sin, lust, desires of the world and live according to God's will? Our old nature should be crucified with Christ Jesus on the cross and experience the resurrection life in Christ Jesus, which is a process that takes place as we walk with God.

THE FATHER'S HEART

Jesus crucifixion is our righteousness which enable us to be able to enter the presence of God because of His blood, His atonement, He will for ever be our righteousness. We must abide in Him that He might dwell in us through His Holly Spirit. The more we walk with Him, the more we are changed by who He is. When we focus on crucifying ourselves, we will never be changed because we are seeing ourselves. That means we are worshiping ourselves instead of beholding Him and whom He is. If we behold Him, we will embrace and be identified with His cross and His resurrection and Christ will become everything in our lives. John 1:1-5 AMP explain that in the beginning was word and the word was with God and the word was God Himself. All things were made and came into existence through him, and without Him there was nothing made that has come into being. In Him was life, and the life was the light of man. And the light shines into the darkness, for the darkness has never overpowered it. He is the message and purpose of the whole creation. When we give ourselves to him, we will gain everything to infinity. We are exchanging the worthless and the death for valuation and a life that cannot be destroyed, which is the best transaction. What is the purpose of being on earth? Why did God create a man and put him on this earth? Is it a coincidence or was there a purpose? The purpose of being on earth is to walk with Him, to have fellowship with Him, to interact with Him and still we can get this original call by exchanging death into indestructible life in Him and to represent him, talk for Him, and to rule the world. He had power to name every living creature and plants.

There is nothing we can do by our strength or knowledge but through the help of the Holy Spirit, we are able. Jesus also said that, He can do nothing by Himself, that why we ought to seek help. In John 5:19, says that, the son can do nothing by himself, he can only do what He sees His Father doing, because whatever the Father does the son also does. We can do nothing without God, the only place where we can get the victory is through Him. We must seek his wisdom and to understand His time. Jesus used the power of heaven in obedient to His Father and as a witness, God gave Him a gift of His Holy Spirit to witness of Him. Luke 9:35, says that, a voice came from the cloud, saying, '' this is my son, my chosen one, listen to Him''. Isaiah 42:1, God had also spoken about Him, ''Here is my servant, whom I uphold, My chosen one, in whom my soul delights. I will put my Spirit on Him, and He will bring justice to the nations.'' Which is also repeated in Matthew 12:18, ''Here is my servant, whom I have chosen, my soul delights. I will put my Spirit on Him, and He will proclaim justice to the nations.'' Revelation 5:3, added that, there was ''no one in heaven and on earth or under the earth, in the realm of the dead and hades, who was able to open the scroll or to take a single look at its contents. Revelation 5:5, added that, 'the Lion of the tribe of Juda, the Root of David has won! He can open the Scroll and break it seven seals!'' Revelation

12:7-9,11 NIV also talks about Him saying, ''and there was war in Heaven, Michael and His Angels fought against the dragon, and the dragon and his angels fought back. But the dragon and his angels were not strong enough, and they lost their place in heaven. That great dragon was hurled down, that ancient serpent called the devil, or Satan, who leads the whole world astray. He was hurled to the earth, and his angels with him. In the same chapter verse 11, says, they overcame by the power of the blood of the lamb (Jesus) and by the word of their testimony, they did not love their lives so much as to shrink from death.

Likewise, there is power behind the blood of the lamb of the Lord and His testimonies which we can use for His purposes and should not be used selfishly. If we use it in a selfish manor, we will end up in shame, frustrated, and even loosing focus. Acknowledging the giver, who is the Father, the Son, and the Holy Spirit, who gives us this exceeding power to use for the benefit of others. The product of using His power selfishly is pride, which always lead to fall. We are called to be seated with Him in the heavenly places, seeing with His eyes, hearing with His ears, and understanding with His heart. Being renewed and carrying His power to the world and collaborating with His Kingdom. Great is His faithfulness and His mercy which are new every morning. Colossians 1:10-11, says, we may live a life worthy of the Lord and please Him in every way, bearing fruits in every good work, growing in the knowledge of God, being strengthened with all power according to His glorious might so that we may have great endurance and patience.

Deuteronomy 8:6, says, we need to walk in His ways and by fearing Him, as it is written that, the fear of the Lord is the beginning of wisdom. Romans 13:13, says, let us behave decently, as in the daytime, not in carousing and drunkenness, not in sexual immorality and debauchery, not in dissension and jealousy but to walk with good work which God prepared ahead of us, (Ephesians 2:10). Jesus said in John 14:12, whoever believes in me will do the works I have been doing, and they will do even greater things than these, because I am going to the Father. He is interceding for us; He has sent a helper, who is the Spirit of God. He has given us grace that our sins will be forgiven. He has also given us a complete armour to protect us from the arrows of the enemy and faith to believe and trust in our master Jesus Christ. That He is not dead, He is alive, and He is coming back to judge the world. Where will you and I be my friend.

Jesus gave a parable of ten virgin, who were invited for a wedding, they took their lamp and went to meet the bridegroom. Five were foolish and five were wise. The foolish one took their lamps but did not take any extra oil. The wise ones, however, took oil in jars along with their lamps. The bridegroom was a long time in coming, and they all became drowsy and fell asleep. At midnight, the cry rang out. Here is the bridegroom! Come out and meet him. Then all the virgin woke up and trimmed their lamp. The foolish ones said to the wise one, give us some of your oil, or our lamp are going out. But they replied no, there may not enough for both of us. Instead, go and buy more for yourselves. But while they were on their way to buy the oil, the bridegroom arrived. The wise virgin went in with him to the wedding banquet and the door was shut. When the foolish one alive, they called lord, lord, open the door for us, but he replied, truly I tell you, I do not know you. Therefore, keep watch, because you do not know the day or hour.

The ten virgins represent the church, we are all invited for wedding of the Lord, each one of us has been given a lamp which is the word of God. And the oil which represent the Holy spirit. We need to be alert, the bible is telling us not to sleep, otherwise we might be found sleeping when the master comes. Sleeping is lack of reading the word of God, praying, which is one way of talking to Him, worshiping, which is one way of connecting with God and inviting the Holy spirit in our heart who is meant to direct, remind, intercede, and advocate for us. He knows the time and the hour that we need to connect with our master, otherwise our physical body is weak, it gets exhausted after our daily chaos and all what come next is sleep, worries, fear, confusion, which steal our heart from the creator to the creation. That's why we always need, first thing in the morning to ask for a helper and last thing before we sleep to protect our mind and heart and for direction.

THE WORK OF THE HOLY SPIRIT

I t is because of the grace; the Lord has given us which is helping us to abide in Him. It is only when we receive the Holy Spirit that the eyes of our heart will be opened. We need to receive the bread of life from our master. According to Luke 24:13-32, two disciples on the way to Emmaus were walking together with Jesus but their eyes were restrained, so that they could not know Him. They were talking about Jesus of Nazareth who was a prophet, mighty indeed, powerful in word before God and all the people. The chief priest and our ruler handed Him over to be sentenced to death, and they crucified Him, but we had hoped that he was one who was going to redeem Israel. And what is more, it is the third day since all this took place. In addition, some women went to the tomb this morning but did not find the body. They said that they found an angel who told them that he is alive. some of our companion went to check and found the same. But Jesus told them how foolish they were and how slow of heart to believe all that the prophet have spoken. Did not the Christ had to suffer these things and then enter his glory? When he was at the table with them, he took the bread, gave thanks, broke it, and began to give it to them. Then their eyes were opened, and they recognised him, and he disappeared from the sight.

They asked each other, were not our hearts burning within us while he talked with us on the road and opened the scriptures to us. Our eyes will open when we invite him to eat with us. Only when we receive our bread directly from him will the eyes of our heart be opened. These two disciples walked with him a long way, talked with him but they could not recognise him until he broke the bread. We cannot recognize him until he breaks the bread. Thomas was like you and me today, he could not believe that Jesus was alive and had been seen by other disciples unless he sees the nail marks in his hand and put his fingers where the nails were, and put his hand into side, he will not believe it. After a week while they were together in the house while the door was locked, Jesus came and stood among them and said, peace be with you. Then he said to Thomas, ''Put your finger here, see my hands. Reach out your hand and put it into my side. Stop doubting and believe. Then Thomas said to Jesus, my Lord, and my God. But Jesus told him, because you have seen me, you have believed, blessed are those who have not seen and yet have believed. The bible says faith is believing in what you do not see. But through his holy spirit he will open our eyes to see him and our ears to hear him. He is a good God, faithful and true, abounding in love, what a mighty God we serve.

THE FATHER'S HEART

The Angels bow before him, heavens adore him, he is mighty in battle and he strengthens us when we are weak. Worship him, glorify his name and great is his faithfulness and he is just and true.

In addition to these, Joel 2:28-32, God says that, ''I will pour my Spirit upon all flesh, and your son and daughters shall prophesy, old men shall dream dreams, young men shall see visions, men servants and maid servants I will pour my spirit. I will show wonders in heavens and earth, blood and fire and columns of smoke. The sun shall be turned into darkness and the moon to blood before the great and terrible day of the lord comes. Whoever shall call on my name, shall be delivered and saved. For in Mount Zion and in Jerusalem there shall be those who, escape, as the Lord has said, and among the remnant, shall be those whom the Lord calls. Enoch prophesied about this day in Jude 14-16, ''See, the lord is coming with thousands of his holy ones to Judge everyone, and to convict all the ungodly acts, they have done in ungodly way, and of all the harsh words ungodly sinners have spoken against Him''. These men are grumblers and faultfinders they follow their own evil desires, they boast about themselves and praise others for their own progress.

Walking with God opens our spiritual ears and eyes to understand and see things the way He understands them. We are changed from the fallen man to a man whom He created in the beginning through His spirit and salvation. You can prophesy, that's why Enoch could see thousands of years to come. God is beyond time; He see from the perspective of eternity and to Him a future is as clear as present. So, if we as a church walk with Him, we will prophesy, and we will be caught up into the Heavens to be with Him. It is possible if Enoch could recover at his time when there was not much hope. In his time the man had been chased from the presence of God with presents of curses. But the man Enoch, ignored all this and decided to seek Him, and he found Him. Today there is hope because God has given us His only begotten son to die on the cross because of our sins, through Him we are redeemed. We have been separated from the anger of the Lord, now is a matter of connecting ourselves with the Father through salvation and seeking His righteousness. As the bible say, seek and you will find, knock and the door shall be opened for you, ask and it shall be given to you. For everyone who asks, receive and everyone who seeks, find and him who knocks, the door shall be opened for him, (Matthew 7:7-8). Enoch searched for Him, he knocked at His door and He opened, he asked, and he was given. He was given every good gift that was given to Adam in the beginning. The man could prophesy, he did not taste the sting of death because the Lord took him, and He was speaking on behalf of God. Man was created to be a representative of God on earth, to speak for Him.

And that's why the Father is working hard to reconcile Himself with the man, as we can see that it is a huge sacrifice to offer His only beloved son to die for a man, as a price to pay our sins, that through Him we have no debt with the devil. We can see His supremacy in Colossians 1:16-20, which affirm that all things were created, that is in heaven, earth, visible or invisible, whether thrones, or dominions, or principalities, or powers, all things were created by him, and for him. He is before all things consist, and He is the head of the body, the church, who is the beginning, the firstborn from the dead, that in all things he might be pre-eminence. For it pleased the Father that in him should all fullness dwell and having made peace through the blood of his cross, by him to reconcile all things unto himself, by him whether things in earth or in heaven. He is called the word of God; his communication is found in everything that was made. That is why John Amos Comenius said, Nature is the God's Second book. The Lord is revealed in everything that was made. He made His creation to speak through it and man was the crowning glory of his creation. He made man in his image to represent him, which include speaking for him. That is why most of the people who walked with God in the scripture prophesied. If we can recover our basic purpose, to walk with God, we will also recover our basic purpose, which is to speak for him.

WHAT IS OUR DESTINY?

There is power in what we choose. Choices in life are very important, they are the ones which determine our destination either successful life or failure, either happiness or sorrows. In the garden of Aden there were two trees. The man had to choose either life or death. There was a time I was praying for our church because my heart desire was when people become members to remain and not to leave. So, my prayer was for the Lord to build a hedge or a spiritual fence, so that whoever comes will never leave, but will remain and worship our God together. I think I heard clearly because our Father did not accept my will. He said anywhere with a fence is a prison, and his will is for every individual to have their own choices. His will is for everyone to have freedom of choice, if their desire is to stay, let the Lord protect them. And God reminded me of Abraham, he gave him the plan, but he had to make a choice, whether to leave his family and follow him or stay.

Joseph had great dreams as a child but through pain and process that he went through, he could have let it go but he retained the faith and trusted in God. His brothers hated him and were jealousy because of his dreams and favour from his father. They wanted to kill him, they put him in a well, lucky enough there was no water. They decided to sell him as a slave to the Egyptians. But the favour of the lord followed him. He became in charge of Potiphar's household and all that he owned; the lord blessed the household of the Egyptian because of Joseph. He was also blessed physically, he was well-built and handsome, which led the wife of his master to admire him. But Joseph refused which led the wife to lie to her husband that he wanted to rape her. His master put him in prison, where the favour of the lord continued. He was put in charge of the prisoners. He could interpret dreams while in prison and that is the place, he met the cup bearer who connected him to the King of Egypt. He managed to interpret a king's dream which promoted him to become a prime minister of Egypt. If Joseph could have focused on the negative and chose not to walk with God, his live could have been very frustrating but instead he made a good choice which made his life remarkably successful.

To connect with God, we need to make the right choices, to choose either life or death. Adam chose death, what are you going to choose? It is not by might not by power but by my spirit says the lord, after we decide, we leave everything to the silversmith who will shape us the way he wants us to be. Joshua told the children of Israel to choose what they want to serve, but as for him and his family he chose to serve the lord. Our master has done a lot for us as a testimony that he loves us now he is telling us, choose what we want life or death. Proverbs 3:5, says, trust in the lord with all your heart and lean not on your own understanding. Jeremiah 33:1-3, is telling us to call unto God and he will answer us and tell us great and unsearchable things we do not know. He is willing to commune with us all what he wants is our attention. He has prepared the process to renew us, to purify and to make us blameless. And the peace of God which transcends all understanding will guard our hearts and minds in Christ Jesus. We need to think whatever is true, noble, right, pure, lovely, admirable and if anything is excellent or praiseworthy. The God of peace will be with us. Understand that we can do all things through Christ who strengthen us. Our destiny is to be redeemed through the blood of the Lamb, through the power of the cross, through the name of Jesus and the power that raised Christ from the dead.

Father there is power when your people walk with you. There is light, wisdom, understanding and knowledge, which are the product of the Holy Spirit. Its only through your power in your Holy Spirit that we can represent you on this earth. Through your presence, light will shine in the darkness, and goodness will overshadow evil, our children will not struggle to live a decent life. Our women will submit to their husband, our men will love their wives the way you love the church. Our homes, schools, communities, town cities, nations, there will be peace, harmony, and love. Everyone will be willing to help where they can. Masters will respect the servants and servants will obey their masters. Let your light shine Lord, you say we are the salt of the earth help us to be tasty so that the world will know that you are with your people.

According to Galatian 5:22-23, confirms that, the words we speak need to have impact, reconciliation, faith, love, joy, peace, and patient, which are the fruit of the Holy Spirit. Luke 6:45 emphasis that, a good man, out of his treasure of his heart brings forth good and the evil man brings forth evil, for his mouth speaks from that which fills his heart. The last day church will walk with God, it will not taste death because the lord will take it, for it will be dying every day to self by walking with God. Jesus said take up your cross and follow me dairy. John Amos Comenius (1592-1670), the Great Didactic, Holland, (1957), wrote about the world today, saying that it is full of various useless things and complicated hooks and the only true peace of mind and soul can be found in the ones heart where Christ the saviour should dwell and rule.

Proverb 16:7, says, when a man way is pleasing to the Lord, he makes even his enemies live at peace with him. That means that there is rest and peace if our ways pleases the master. It continues to say better a little with righteousness than much gain with injustice. In our heart we plan, but the lord determines our steps. Honest scales and balances are from the Lord, all the weights in the bag are of his making. And the Kings detest wrongdoing, for the throne is established through righteousness. So, faithfulness and humbling ourselves to our master is the only key of a successful life. Isaiah 60 says, sons and daughters arise and shine, for your light has come and the glory of the lord rises upon you. See, darkness covers the earth and thick darkness is over the peoples, but the Lord rises upon you and his glory appears over you. Nations will come to your light, and Kings to the brightness of your dawn. Lift your eyes and look about you. All assemble and come to you, your sons come from far, and your daughters are carried on the arm. Then you will look and be radiant, your heart will throb and well with joy, the wealth on the seas will be brought to you, to you the riches of the nations will come.

See darkness covers the earth, and thick darkness over the people. Wars, diseases with no cure, men hating each other, men becoming too greedy, too selfish, poverty, unnecessary killing, but the lord is giving us the hope. His glory appears over you, nations will come to your light and kings to the brightness of your dawn. Lift your eyes and about you, your sons come from far and your daughters are carried on the arm. Then you will look and be radiant, your heart will throb and swell with Joy, the wealth of the seas will be brought to you, herds of camels will cover your land, young camels of Midian and Ephah. And all from Sheba will come to you bearing Gold and incense and proclaiming to praise the Lord. foreigners will rebuild your walls, and Kings will serve you. Though in anger I struck you, in favour I will show compassion. This is a reward of the Lord when we come back to Him and repent and start walking with Him. He is proving to be a provider, protector, joining, peace giver, and to be the light and the healer of the land. If only we will surrender ourselves to Him. He is saying in Matthew 11:28, come to me, all of you who are weary and carrying heavy loads, and I will give you rest. `

HOW CAN WE WALK WITH GOD?

W e will never be perfect, but God will always be perfect. He will work in us to align us in His will. All what He need is our desire, to choose His way and to focus on Him, our hearts should work together with Him, while walking with Him. We cannot carry along our old life choices and habits. Noah chose to live a Godly life according to, (Genesis 6:8), he was filled with faith while being surrounded by a very evil world. He trusted Gods words; out of faith he built a massive ark in an area that was completely land locked. He did everything that God asked him to do. He was obedient, faithful, and even when conditions appeared absurd to those around him. All what the Father needs is obedient and receptive heart. Noah walked with God, alone, people around him did not understand him. They thought he was mental, laughed at him and being overlooked but when the rain came, he was the only one who was saved with his family.

Moses loved God and he could talk with God, but he thought the task that the Lord was giving him was too difficult, and it was, in our human viewpoint, but to God all things are possible. Moses had to be trained by God Himself, encouraged and demonstrated His power to him. God asked him, "Moses what do you have", Moses answered, "a rod", God told him, "cast it on the ground", and the rod changed into a serpent, a symbol of royal and divine power worn on the crown of the pharaohs, and Moses fled from it with fear. God also told him, "put your hand into your bosom", and his hand became leprous, as white as snow, finally God told him to change the water to blood, if they will not belief the first testimony they will belief the second , if not the second they will belief the third one. Moses asked God, "Father, do you know I am slow in speech, and a heavy and awkward tongue. How will I communicate with your people?" And the lord said to him, "who has made man's mouth, or who makes the dumb, or deaf, or dumb, seeing, or blind, is not I, the Lord? Now go I will be your mouth and will teach you what you shall say." But Moses requested Him to send another person. Then the anger of the Lord blazed against Moses; He said, "is there not Aaron your brother, the Levite? I know he can speak well, and he is coming out to meet you, and when he sees you, he will be overjoyed. You must speak to him and put the words in his own mouth; and I will be with your mouth, and with his mouth and I will teach you what you shall do. He shall be your mouthpiece and you shall be as his God to him" (Exodus 4).

Some time we think God does not know us, whom we are and what we are going through. Corresponding to the conversation between Moses and God, He did not need any introduction, he could have told Moses I knew you before you were born. But He preferred to say who gives tongue, ears, and eyes, I Am the creator. Look at your hand Moses, I can change it the way I want, look at your rod, you think it is dead, but I can make it life and start moving and it can be a dangerous weapon as well, which you can fear. I AM GOD, THE CREATER OF THE UNIVERSE. Through my words, everything changes, we can be changed, and be what he created us to be if we desire. He told Moses I have heard the cry of my people. When you are praying, He is hearing your crying. You may think you have come to a dead end, but by his one word everything can turn around. He is a good God, full of mercy, abounding in love, faithful, just, and true.

God is patient to each one of us, He was patient with Moses, He takes time to transform us from the fallen man, full of flesh to whom He want us to be. All what He want is for us to work together with Him by renewing our mind, He will never leave us or forsake us. 1 Timothy 1:12-17, God through His mercy Has judged and counted Paul faithful and trustworthy, appointing him to be steward in His ministry although he was formerly blaspheming, persecuting, shamefully, outrageously and aggressively insulting to Him, nevertheless, he obtained mercy because he acted out of ignorance in unbelief. And the grace of our lord Jesus flowed out superabundantly and beyond measure for him, accompanied by faith and love that are in Christ Jesus. He confirmed the saying, that Christ Jesus came into the world to save sinners of whom Paul was foremost, which is sure and true, worthy, and universal acceptance. If Paul found mercy, the foremost of all sinners, even us today Jesus Christ will show forth and display all his perfect forgiving and patient, to encourage us to believe on Him to gain eternal life. May the King of eternity, incorruptible and immortal, invisible the only God, be honoured and His Glory for ever and ever, Amen. Through Him, Paul assured that we can be changed, saved, which is sanctification, we can be renewed, shaped, which is justification. He can entrust us into a service in His kingdom after strengthening and enabling us. He is a God full of mercy, faithful, and true and He is omnipresent. He will give us a task which He will also participate. 1 Thessalonians 2:4, God entrust us with the glad tidings, so you will not speak of men but to please God, who tests the heart? The Holy Spirit will guide us, give us comfort, and teaches us according to the full mercy of God. He will never leave us nor forsake us.

God is always trying to draw us to Him. He desires to walk with us daily and He wants our life to be transformed into joyful relationship with Him, regardless of the circumstances we might be living in. He wants to hear our concerns, hopes, dreams, struggles and thanking Him for who He is and the work He has done in our lives. We also need to ask for His direction upon our life consistently, humbling ourselves to seek His will. Walking with Him will build confidence, courage, gain wisdom, knowledge and understanding, hating what is evil and clinging toward the goal. Acts 4:13, says that, when the magistrates, elders, scribes, Annas the high priest and Caiaphas, John, Alexander and others who belonged to the high priestly relationship saw their boldness and independent, expressiveness of Peter and John and recognised that they were common men with no educational advantages, they marvelled; and they knew that they had been with Jesus. Our character will change, the way we think, the way we plan, making decision will change and the way we speak, by seeking God guidance, patient, perseverance and trusting the author and the finisher of our faith. Our actions and choices will align with Gods will, meditating his words daily and desiring to please Him, avoiding bad choices and habits.

The advantages of walking with God is that, the spirit of the living God will live in you. According to Galatians 5:22-23, asserts that we will bear fruits of the spirit, which is love, joy, peace, forbearance, kindness, goodness, faithfulness, gentleness, and self-control. Against such things there is no law. The bible tells us that we will be the salt of the earth, salt makes food tasty and it can heal a wound. So, wherever you go through the presence of God will be healing and the life of people will change from tasteless to sweetness. We are the light of the world, when it is dark, you cannot see clearly, but when the light shines you can see. When the eyes are perfect you can differentiate between good and bad, which will help to make good choices. God's glory will shine on us to illuminate where we are, so that the people around us can see clearly. What a powerful God He is. We will be able to stand out, act different and shine brighter and know him better. He will open our eyes to see, our ears to hear and to know His plan and purpose. We should welcome Him every morning, because He says His mercies are new every morning and great is His faithfulness. He will give us direction and wisdom to face each day a flesh. According to Colossians 1:10, Paul is saying that we should walk according in a manner worth pleasing to God and bearing fruits in every good work and growing in the knowledge of God.

Jeremiah 18:6--, God is talking to us today, ''O my people, can I not do with you as this potter does?'' Like clay in hand of a potter, so are you in my hand, O my people. If at any time I announce a nation or a Kingdom is to be uprooted, torn down and destroyed, and if that nation I warned repents of its evil, then I will relent and not inflict on it the disaster I had planned. And if at another time I announce that a nation or a Kingdom is to be build or planted, and if it does evil in my sight and does not obey me, then I will reconsider the good I had intended to do for it. When the pot in the potter's hand was marred in his hands, he formed it into another pot, shaping it as seemed best to him. We are clay in the potter's hand; he can shape us according to the way he wants us to be, but God values us more than clay because He is giving us choices to make. He is giving us warning through prophets, His own son, preachers, evangelist, missionaries, media, books, Bible, and the rest. He is saying, repent come to me and I will give you rest. In Revelation 22:7-- Jesus is saying, Behold, I am coming soon! Blessed is he who keeps the words of the prophecy in this book. Behold, I am coming soon! My reward is with me, and I will give to everyone according to what he has done. I am the Alpha and the Omega, the first and the last, the Beginning, and the End. Blessed are those who wash their robes, that they may have the light to the tree of life and may go through the gates into the city. For outside are the dogs, those who practise magic arts, the sexually immoral, the murderer, the idolaters and everyone who loves and practices falsehood. I, Jesus have sent my angel to give you this testimony for the churches. I am the root and the offspring of David, and the bright Morning Star.

The Spirit and the Bride say, 'COME!!,' and let him, whoever is thirsty, let him come, and whoever wishes, let him take the gift of water of life. We are all called, we have all been forgiven through the power of the cross, through the blood of Jesus and the name that is above every name which every knee shall bow and every tongue confess that he is the son of God. We have been invited to this new creation that the Creator is putting back to clay and moulding again to be new creation that is not contaminated by the sin of the world. Come, everyone, a choice and a desire are the only qualification that is needed. There is a river of the water of life, as clear as crystal, flowing from the throne of God and of the lamb, down the middle of the great street of the city. On each side of the river stood tree of life, bearing twelve crops of fruits, yielding it fruits every month. And the leaves of the tree are for healing of the nations. No longer will there be any curse. The throne of God and the Lamb will be in the city, and his servants will serve him. They will see his face, and his name will be on their foreheads. There will be no more night. They will not need light of a lamp or the light of the sun for the Lord God will give them light. And they will reign for ever and ever. These words are trustworthy and true. The Lord, the God of the spirits of the prophets, sent his Angel to show his servants the things that must soon take place.

WHAT DOES IT TAKE TO WALK WITH GOD?

G od's love is beyond our human understanding, Jesus gave a parable of the prodigal son, to explain in a human way the love of the father. The way we can understand better. He narrates a story of a man who had two sons. The younger son demanded the share of the estate, and his father divided his property between them. The younger son got together all he had and went to a distant country and squandered his wealth in wild living. After spending everything, there came a severe famine in that whole country, and he began to be in need. So, he went and was hired by a citizen of that country to his field to feed pigs. He longed to eat the pods that pigs were eating but was not given. When he came to his senses, he thought how many of his father's servants have food to spare, and here I am starving to death. '' I will go back to my father and say, I have sinned against heaven and against you. I am no longer worthy to be called your son; make me like one of your hired servants.'' So, he got up and went to his father, but to his surprise while he was still a long way off, his father saw him and was filled with compassion for him, he ran to his son, threw his arms around him, and kissed him. As dirty as he was, the father's love is beyond our human perspective. The son said to the father, '' father, I have sinned against heaven and against you. I am no longer worthy to be called your son.'' But to everyone amazement the father ordered a robe, a ring, and sandals to be put on him. To make the matter worse, the fattened calf to be slaughtered to celebrate, for this son who was dead and now is alive, he was lost and is found. That is how much the Father loves us, any time we fall, come back and surrender, His arms are always open to receive us. He does not count or deal with our past his mercies are new every morning, great is his faithfulness. It does not matter what you have done, just go back, he is waiting for you ready to receive you. His love is not twisted or measured by what he hears or see, it is 100% unconditional. It is permanent but you must make a choice to leave the distant land and go back, He is waiting for you. Matthew 11: 28-30, Jesus is saying, ''come to me those who are weary and burdened, and I will give you rest. Take my yoke upon you and learn from me, for I am gentle and humble in heart, and you will find rest for your soul. For my yoke is easy and my burden is light. Because all things had been committed to me by my Father. While you are back, keep on obeying, keeping your step with his, modelling your actions after His, following His instruction, walking with harmony, unity, peace, love, liberty, and communion with Him. He will open doors, gates, break walls that are hindering and open new path that you never knew that they existed. Stop desiring your inheritance before time, have patience, there is time for everything.

Isaiah 40:3-5, is saying, a voice is calling in the desert, where we are today. Prepare the way for the Lord, let us open or heart for the Lord. Make straight in the wilderness a highway for our God. Every valley shall be raised up and every mountain and hill made low. The rough ground shall become level and the rugged places a plain. And the glory of the lord will be revealed, and all mankind together will see. For the mouth of the lord has spoken. The sick will be healed, blind will see, lame will walk, there will be peace, His presence will be a wall for his people like the way Jerusalem is surrounded by mountains. In additional to this He is saying in Isaiah 45, that through Jesus Christ our Lord, He will subdue nations, strip Kings of their armour, open doors, gates will not shut, level mountains, breakdown gates of bronze and cut through bars of iron. I will give you the treasures of darkness, reaches stored in secret places, so that you may know that I am the Lord, the God of Israel, who summons you by name. I summon you by name and bestow on you a title of honour. I am the Lord, and there is no other, apart from me there is no other God. I will strengthen you, so that from the rising of the sun to the setting, men may know there is none beside me. I am the Lord and there is no other. I form the light and create darkness; I bring prosperity and create disaster. I the LORD DO ALL THIS THINGS. You, heaven above, rain down righteousness, let the clouds shower it down. Let the earth open wide, let salvation springs up, let righteousness grow with it, I the LORD have created it.

Isaiah 58:12, if you walk with me your ancient ruins shall be rebuilt, you shall raise up the foundation of many generations, you shall be called the repairer of the breach, the restorer of streets to dwell in. Our good foundation of morals is damaged, it is not there, from our sons and daughters, husband and wives, neighbourhood, and nations. God want us to fight for them and to encourage people to participate in building the ruined wall. As in the time of Nehemiah, when he received the message about the wall of Jerusalem and the gates have been burned with fire. He sat down and wept. For some days he mourned and fasted and prayed before the God of heaven, O Lord, God of heaven, the great and awesome God, who keeps his covenant of love with those who love him and obey his commands, let your ear be attentive and your eyes open to hear the prayers of your servant before you, day and night for your servants, the people of Israel. I confess we have done; we have acted wickedly towards you. We have not obeyed the commands, decrees, and laws you gave your servant Moses. You told Moses if we are unfaithful you will scatter us among the nations, but if we come back to you and obey your commands, then even if we are exiled, you will gather us to the place you have chosen as a dwelling of your name. We are your people, whom you redeemed by your great strength and mighty hand.

This is the prayer that we need for our foundation is destroyed, walls and the gates are not existing, people are doing what they want. There is no fear of God, not mentioning the law, we know more that we do not even need to seek God for wisdom. Forgive us lord, we stand in the gap for our children, your people, and nations, forgive us Lord for not obeying you and not walking according to your will. We do what pleases our heart, running from one God to the other, trying to seek for peace which can only be found in you. Forgive Lord, our children are killing each other, drug addicted, alcohol addicted, they are not even respecting us or listening to our instruction. We are also too busy for them, forgive us Lord, the demand of house bills, mortgages and maintenance are overwhelming, we cannot rest. So, the enemy is using this as an advantage to visit our children when we are at work to gloom them in selling and taking drugs. Have mercy upon us lord, we need you more than anything, more than ever before, otherwise we do not have tomorrow generation. There is a spirit that is breaking marriages, for many years, there had not been an outbreak of marriage separation like now. We need you Lord, the bible says, a house divided cannot stand against itself and is brought into desolation. How can we help our children if we do not have a foundation in ourselves? Children are confused, in fact they are saying most of the crime are being found in children who are being brought up by single mothers. Have mercy Lord hold the marriages and build walls of protection on the single mothers and their children. We are your servants, Lord! Hear our cries. Do something new in our lives, yesterday is gone, and another day has come, do something new in our lives.

James 4:7, says, submit yourself to God, resist the devil and he will free from you. It is important to keep on reminding ourselves that our enemy the devil or Satan is not figment of imagination, a legend, or superstitious belief. He is real spiritual being, who leads a host of fallen angels and demons that make up a kingdom of darkness. So, we must resist him. Ephesians 6:10--, Paul is telling us to be strong in the Lord and draw our strength from Him. He is encouraging us to put on God's armour of a heavy-armed soldier which God supplies, that we may be able successfully to stand up against all the strategies and the deceits of the devil. For we are not wrestling with flesh and blood but against the authoritarianism, against the powers, against the world rulers of this present darkness, against the spirit forces of wickedness in the heavenly realm. Therefore, put on God's complete armour that you may be able to resist and stand your ground on the evil day, and, having done all, stand, firmly in your place. Stand therefore having tightened the belt of truth around your loins and put on the breastplate of righteousness in place, and with your feet fitted with the readiness that comes from the gospel of peace. In addition to all this, take up the shield of faith, with which to extinguish all the flaming arrows of the evil one. Take the helmet of salvation and the sword of the spirit, which is the word of God. And pray in the spirit on all occasion with all kinds of prayers and requests. To that end keep alert and watch with strong purpose and perseverance and interceding on behalf of the saints, be alert and always keep on praying for all saints. Revelation 12, John is also talking about who the devil is, so brothers and sisters we have a master who is beyond every forces that we can imagine, He is God of gods, King of kings, Majesty, Lord of heaven leaving in us. All what we need is just to connect with Him, trust Him, and walk with Him, He is a wonderful counsellor, Mighty warrior, great in battle, Jehovah is His name. God of Abraham, Isaac and Jacob, worship Him, adore Him, in you Lord we trust.

Romans 8:28-39, Paul is saying that all things work together for good of those who love Him, who have been called according to his purpose. For those God foreknew he also predestined to be conformed to the likeness of his Son, that he might be the firstborn among many brothers. And those he predestined, he also called, and those he called, he also justified, those he justified, he also glorified. In response to this if God is for us who can be against us? He who did not spare his own Son but gave him up for us all, how will he not also, along with him, graciously give us all things? Who will bring any charge against those whom God has chosen? It is God who justifies. Who is he that condemns? Christ Jesus, who died, and more than that, he was raised to life, he is at the right hand of God and is also interceding for us. Who shall separate us from the love of Christ? Shall trouble or hardship or persecution or famine or nakedness or danger or sword? As it is written, for your sake we face death all day long, we are considered as sheep to be slaughtered. But in all these things we are more than conquerors through him who loved us. For neither death nor life, neither angels nor demons, neither the present nor future, nor any powers, neither height nor depth, nor anything else in all creation, will be able to separate us from the love of God that is in Christ Jesus our Lord.

HOW CAN WE OVERCOME DISTRACTIONS?

O ur sinful nature despite of our natural freedom, too often we misuse this freedom and engage in behaviour that is inconsistence with God's love and even with our desire to live faithfully within our limited understanding of His love. Consequently, too often we practice immorality, impurity, idolatry, hostility, quarrelling, anger, dissension, envy, and other behaviours of not loving neighbours as ourselves. That is why we need the presence of the Holy Spirit in our hearts. He produces the fruits in our lives to sweeten us and those around us. There will be joy, peace, patient, kindness, love, goodness, faithfulness, gentleness, and self-control. Against such things there is no law. Our past, shame can become a problem, worries, anxiousness and sin.

According to Hebrews 12: 1-3, we are surrounded by such a great cloud of witnesses, we should throw off everything that is obstructing and the sin that is easily ensnaring on us. The unnecessary weight or things that are blocking our ways so that we can run with perseverance the race marked out for us, fixing our eyes on Jesus, the pioneer and perfecter of our faith. For He endured the cross because of the joy set before Him, He endured the scorning, its shame, and now He is sitting at the right side of the throne of God. When we focus our eyes on Him, He who endured such opposition from sinners, we will not grow weary and lose heart. The things that distract our walk with God must go, especially the sin that so easily entangle us. If you can imagine having a friend when you are walking together, who is not focusing on you, is not listening or talking with you, only concentrating on the phone, talking to other people or on face book rather than interacting with you. You will not enjoy the walk and you cannot go far. The same thing can affect our walk with the Father if we cannot focus on Him. Sometime even good things can distract if they are overly done without thinking or planning. For example, work and earning money, watching the tv, face book, clubbing if they are overly done, they can lead to obsession, work is good, but if it will make us neglect our families, relationship with God, can become a distraction.

We need time to read the word of God, prayers, and worship Him. The word of God is like a map to His kingdom, it will guide us to His ways, because our ways are not His way. Prayer is personal connection with Him. The bible is telling us to ask and it will be given to us, seek and you will find, knock and the door will be opened for you. We also need to praise Him, He is our redeemer, mighty warrior, great in battle, Jehovah is His name. Jehovah Jireh, He is our provider. He is our salvation, our righteousness, our faith, and our peace and joy. He is good all the time. He is the God who created heaven and earth. He is the same yesterday, today and forever. He is the Alpha and Omega, beginning and the end.

John 14:15-18, Jesus is saying that if we love Him, we will obey what He commands. And He will ask the Father, and He will give us another Councillor to be with us for ever, the Spirit of truth. He says that the world cannot accept him because it neither sees him nor knows Him. But we know Him, for He lives with us and will be in us. He will not leave us like orphans, He will come to us through His Holy Spirit. The world will not see Him, but we will see Him because He lives, we will also live. If we have His commands and obeys them, we show the love for Him. And if we love Him, we will be loved by His Father, and He will also love us and will show Himself to us. John 16:7-33, Jesus is saying that it is for good that He is going away. Unless He goes away, the counsellor will not come to us, but if he goes, He will send Him to us. And when the Holy Spirit come He will convict the world of the guilt in regard to sin and righteousness and judgement, in regard to sin, because men do not believe in Jesus, in regard to righteousness, because He is going to the Father. And regarding judgement, the prince of this world now stands condemned. The Holly Spirit of truth when He comes, He will guide us into all truth. He will speak not his own but only what He hears, and he will also tell us what to come. He will bring Glory to Jesus by taking from what is for Him and making it known to us. Everything that belong to the Father is for Jesus. That's why he says, the spirit will bring what is His and make it known to us. My Father will give us whatever we ask in His name, if we ask, we will receive, and our joy will be complete. The Father loves us because we love Jesus and have believed that He came from God. Jesus says in Him we will have peace but, in the world, we will have trouble. But, let us have courage, He has overcome the world.

Holy Spirit brings the power of God and the love of Jesus in each one of us, individually, which manifest in our beings and therefore become the directive of our action, because our souls long to be directed away from destructions. But our nature is sinful, despite our inherent freedom, too often we engage in behaviour that is inconsistence with our desire to live faithfully within our limited understanding of His love. Therefore, too often we practice behaviours that are not pleasing to God, for example, immorality, impurity, idolatry, hostility quarrelling, anger, dissension, envy, and not loving our neighbours as ourselves. That's why we daily need the presence of the Holy Spirit in our hearts. He produces the fruits in our lives, love, peace, joy, patience, kindness, and self-control. Through the power of the Holy Spirit Elijah who was a prophet of God, in 11Kings 18, prayed for the fire of God to fall and burn the sacrifice and the fire fell and consumed, the sacrifice, the wood, stones and the soil, and also licked up the water in the trench. After this He slaughtered 450 prophets of Baal in the valley of Kishon.

Through the power of the Holy Spirit Peter stood in Act 2 and preached the word and three thousand believed. Although he had given up and started fishing, when the Holy Spirit came upon them, he had power and courage to stand and proclaim the word of the Lord. He said save yourself from corrupt generation and baptised those who accepted the message. Joshua was told by God in Joshua 1:6, be strong and courageous, because you will lead this people to inherit the land, I swore to their forefathers to give them. Be careful to obey all the law, my servant Moses gave to you, do not turn on your right or left, that you may be successful wherever you go. Do not let the book of the law depart from your mouth, meditate on it day and night, so that you may be careful to do everything written in it. Then you will be prosperous and successful. Have I not commanded you? Be strong and courageous. Do not be terrified, do not be discouraged, for the Lord your God will be with you wherever you go.

The presence of God in our lives is important because man without God is weak, and sometimes we fear the known and unknown. Moses feared his own people, Pharaoh and all his past was hunting him. Today we may look at it and sea weak Moses but as a human, all his past was too much for him. He had run away as a murderer, the people he was trying to save were against him. The Pharaoh he was going to face in the man who brought him up and is the man he ran away from. But in Deuteronomy 1:21, the same man Moses is sending the men to spy out the land and is telling them, do not be afraid, do not be discouraged. Fear is a strong weapon of preventing us from moving forward. It is a wall that imprisons us, we think we are free, but fear is all over holding us, what will happen, what will people say and what about if I fail. All these are strongholds and roadblocks. 1 John 4:18, is telling us there is no fear in love, the perfect love drives out fear, because fear has to do with punishment. The one who fears is not made perfect in love. So, if we connect ourselves with God through His Spirit, His love will consume all our fears, and there will be peace, joy, and love.

Worry is another monster in our lives, but in Matthew 6:25-34, Jesus is saying, stop being worried about life, food, or our bodies, what to wear. Life is greater than food or clothing. The birds of the air neither sow nor reap nor gather into burns, and yet our heavenly Father keeps feeding them. Are we not more worthy than the birds? And who by worrying and being anxious can add one unit of measure to his stature or to the spun of his life? Consider the lilies of the field and learn thoroughly how they grow, they neither toil nor spin, yet, even Solomon in all his magnificence was not arrayed like one of them. If God can dress a grass of the field, which today is alive and green and tomorrow is tossed into the furnace, will He not much more surely cloth you, o you of little faith? Father give us more faith to trust and walk with you. Therefore King Jesus is telling us not to worry and not to be anxious about anything, for the gentiles or heathen wish and crave and diligently seek all these things, and your heavenly Father knows well that you need them all. 'But', seek or aim at, strive after, the kingdom of God and His righteousness first and then all these things taken together will be given you besides. So, do not worry or be anxious about tomorrow, for tomorrow will have worries and anxieties of its own. Each day has enough trouble of its own. In Philippians 4:6,7, Paul is telling us not to fret or have any anxiety about anything, but in every circumstance and in everything by prayer and petition, with thanksgiving, to continue making our request known to God. And the peace of God which transcends all our understanding, will guard our hearts and our minds in Christ Jesus.

Shame is another stronghold that prevent us from moving forward. Exodus 32:25--, when Moses saw that the people were unruly and unrestrained, for Aaron had let them get out of control, so they were a derision and object of shame among their enemies. So, he stood in the gate of the camp, and said, whoever is on the Lords side, let him come to me.

THE FATHER'S HEART

And all the Levites gathered with him. And he said to them, thus says the lord God of Israel, every man put your sword on your side and go in and out from the gate to gate throughout the camp and slay every man his brother, and every man his companion, and every man his neighbour. And about three thousand people fell that day. And because of their obedience they were consecrated as priests to the lord. The next day Moses went to the Lord to make atonement for their sins. God forgave them and said His Angel will go before them. But He sent a Prague upon them because they made the calf to worship. God called them a stiff-necked people! Shame is connected with our sins which disconnect us from the presence of God and we become vulnerable to our enemies because we do not have protection, the confidence and courage disappears and leaves us frustrated and ashamed of every abuse that we receive on the process but this is the reason why our Lord and saviour Jesus Christ died for us. To set us free from the captivity of shame. To wash us with His precious blood and to anoint us with the oil of His Holy Spirit. He is a good God; he gives us grace to hold His anger. Just imagine in the time of Moses if it were today the world could have been empty. For we sin every minute of our life but his grace is sufficient, any time we go back to Him like the prodigal son and repent His love is beyond measure He is ready to forgive and welcome us back home. He is saying your sins are no more, there is no more condemnation to those who belief, they are bloted out, so, we should forget our past and start a new life with Christ Jesus our saviour. Enjoy His presence, worship and honour Him and he will make us the light and the salt of the earth. When the light come the darkness disappear.

Fear is another weapon that distract us from being powerful in Christ Jesus. But this is the word of our God in Isaiah 43:1--, he who created you, fear not, for I have redeemed you, I have summoned you by name, you are mine. When you pass through the waters, I will be with you, and when you pass through the rivers, they will not sweep over you. When you walk through the fire, you will not be burned, and frames will not set you ablaze. For I am the Lord, your God, the Holy One of Israel, your Saviour. I give Egypt for your ransom, Cush and Seba in your stead. Since you are precious and honoured in my sight, and because I love you, I will give men in exchange for your life. Do not be afraid, for I am with you, I will bring your children from the east and gather you from the west. I will say to the north, ''Give them up!'' and to the south, ''Do not hold them back!'' This is what the Lord says, He who made a way through the sea, and a path through the waters, who drew out the chariots and horses, the army and reinforcements together, and lay there, never to rise again, extinguished, snuffed out like wick.

Forget the former things, do not dwell on the past. See I Am doing a new thing! Now it springs up, do you not perceive it? I am making a way in the desert, and streams in wasteland, the wild animals honour me, the jackals and the owls, because I provide water in the desert and streams in the wasteland, to give drink to my people, my chosen, the people I formed for myself, that they may proclaim my praise.

WHAT IS THE OUTCOME?

If we walk with God, he will protect us from our enemies, direct us into the right direction and provide, in our time of need. We have many examples and testimonies in the bible that prove him to be everything that we need, water coming from the rock, red sea parting and there was a highway in the sea and the children of Israel enjoying the walk in it while the Egyptians were swallowed by the same sea at the same time. Food raining from heaven, the manna and children of Israel went with their basket to pick and meat was brought to them when they demanded. God can do great and mighty things in our life if only we can obey and walk with Him. In psalm 91, the psalmist is saying, if we dwell in the shelter of the most high, we will rest in the shadow of the almighty. He will be our refuge and our fortress, our God, in whom I trust. He will save us from the fowler's snare and from deadly pestilence. He will cover us with His feathers, and under his wing we will find refuge. His faithfulness will be our shield and wall. We will not fear the terror of night, nor the arrow that flies by day, nor the pestilence that follows in the darkness, nor the plague that destroy at midday. A thousand may fall at our side, ten thousand at our right hand but it will not come near us. we will only observe with our eyes and see the punishment of the wicked.

If we make the most high our dwelling, no harm will befall us, no disaster will come near our tent, for He will command His Angels concerning us, to guard us in all our ways, they will lift us up in their hands so that we will not strike our foot against a stone. We will tread upon the lion and the cobra; we will trample the great lion and serpent because we love our God the creator of the universe. He will recue us, protect us, for we acknowledge His name. When we call, He will answer, He will be with us in trouble, and will deliver us and honour us. And moreover, He is promising to satisfy us with long life and show us His salvation. These are the great promises of God to us, He says that He is yes and Amen. No word from His mouth will fall without producing something. He says they are like rain which fall on the earth and make the seed grow and we have the harvest. So, if we trust in His word and walk with Him, there is safety, rest, and provision.

We also need to Pay attention to His providence, for example, when Abraham was old, he called his servant in Genesis 24:7-22, he told him the lord God of heaven who took him from his father's house, from the land of his family and birth, who spoke to him and swore to him, saying, ''I will give this land to your offspring, will send his Angel before you and will take a wife for my son Isaac from there.' 'So, the servant left to search a wife for Isaac as he was instructed by his father Abraham. It was a very hard task but through trusting God believing that he can provide he had a strong hope. Timing and praying and trusting God is also essential; the servant went to the well at the time of evening when women go out to draw water. And he prayed, ''God of my master Abraham, I pray you cause me to meet with good success today, and show kindness to my master Abraham, see I stand here by the well of the water, and the daughters of the men of the city are coming to draw water. Let it so be that the girl to whom I say, I pray you, let down your jar that I drink also, let her be the one whom you have selected and appointed and indicated for your servant Isaac to his wife and by it, I shall know that you have shown kindness and faithfulness to my master.''

And before he finishes his prayers, Rebekah, who was a daughter of Bethuel son of Milcah, who the wife of Nahor was the brother of Abraham with her water jar on her shoulder came to fetch the water. The girl was very beautiful and attractive, chaste, and unmarried. She went down to the well, filled her jar and came up. The servant run to meet her and said, '' I pray you, let me drink a little water from your water jar.'' And she offered saying, '' drink, my lord and she quickly let down her jar onto her hand and gave him a drink. She also offered to feed the camel. She was running while feeding the camel and the man was gazing at her in silent, waiting to know if the Lord had made his trip prosperous. He took a gold ring and two bracelets and gave them to her which meant that she has been chosen to be the wife of Isaac.

This story teaches us how to pray and trust that God is listening when we pray. Being patient and seeking God guidance in our life is important. Listening with our spiritual ears, will help us to understand Gods instructions, even little things like water to drink, feeding camel and how willingly the girl was while feeding the camels. She was running, she did not ask for help, she was full of love toward the servant as well as the camels.

If you walk with God, there is harmony between you and God. If you walk according to His instruction, you will remain in spiritual connection. There will be love, personal love and a love for God. We have a master key, the key of David, which can be used to open every door. Jesus said I am the way the truth and the life. John 10:27-28, Jesus said my sheep hear my voice, and I know them, and they follow me. And I give them eternal life; and they shall never perish, neither shall any man pluck them out of my hand. Do not listen to any voice, interact with those who are ready to listen and talk with the voice of the master. Support each other, God uses people to guide your steps. Keep walking no matter how many times you trip and stumble, dust yourself off and continue walking. God will never turn you away, even if you temporarily lose sight of the road, seek for guidance, continue to travel. Walking with God is deciding that God will always hold your hand. Psalm 121:2-8, our help will come from the lord, who made heaven and earth, he will not let your foot slip or be moved; He who keeps you will not slumber. Behold, He who keeps Israel will neither sleep, nor slumber. The lord is your keeper your shade on your right hand. The sun shall not smite you by day or the moon by night. The lord will keep you from all evil, He will keep your life. He will keep your going out and your coming in from this time and forth and forever more. Amen.

Our relationship with God is not just a feeling, it is deeper. Sometimes we feel as if God is too far or too busy. But psalm 34:18, says, the lord is close to the broken hearted and saves those who are crushed in the spirit. Sometime our feelings lie to us. God is accessible and listening to us all the time. Satan is the father of lies and so we need to focus on the truth to sort out fact from fiction. We need to pray before reading the bible. The Holy Spirit helps us focus and to hear what He is placing on our heart with his word. He is the most important member in the family. It is important to spend time with Him. Ask God how He would like to use you and make it a desire. Sharing Jesus with others can brighten your life and others. The Gospel speak for itself, just say it, then God will do the rest. Charles

Spurgeon asserted that, 'gospel is like a caged lion, it does not need to be defended. It simply needs to be let out of its cage.'' Let the Lord use you as a vessel to uncage the lion.

According to Micah 6:8, the lord desire is to walk with us, and this is the purpose of the creation however sin separated man from God according to Genesis 3:8. Romans 5:12 asserts that sin separated humanity from God, but John 14:16-17 gives a hope, courage, strong and confidence because the master Jesus came to restore and forgive through his sacrifice. Now we can have a new relationship with God and become the most important thing in life. We need to seek, knock, and ask, He is promising to be found, and will open the door, and whatever you ask will be given to you. Spend time with Him, let Him be a friend always, in season and out of season, talk to Him throughout the day. Amos 3:3, is challenging us, whether two can walks together except they make an appointment and agree. He adds in verse 7, that the lord God will do nothing without revealing His secret to His servants the prophets. This open our eyes to see that if we allow ourselves to walk with Him, He will reveal His secret to us, He will transform us more and more into His image.

Which is confirmed in 11 Corinthians 5:17, that we are now a new creation, the old is gone. We are walking with the master Jesus through His spirit. 11 Corinthians 3:18, assures that we are being transformed into His very own image in ever increasing splendour and from the lord who is the spirit. Ephesians 1:13-14, maintain that, we are stamped with the seal of the long promised Holy Spirit. The Spirit is the guarantee of our inheritance, the first fruit, the pledge, and indication, the down payment on our inheritance, expectation of its full redemption and our obtaining complete possession of it to the praise of His glory. So, let us strip off and throw aside every burden or unnecessary weight and that sin that so much entangles us, and let us run with patience the appointed course to the race that is set before us. There is a cost in walking with God, Matthew 7:13-14, notes that we have to cut things out of our life that keep us from walking in the ways of God, because we are motivated by His love and a desire to be close to Him.

BENEFIT OF WALKING
WITH GOD

If we trust in the lord and do good, we will dwell in the land and enjoy safe pasture. If we delight ourselves in the lord, He will give us the desires of our heart. For evil men will be cut off, but those who hope in the Lord will inherit the land. We need to trust God in every step we make meditating His word, filling our mind with thoughts of hope and faith. Isaiah 30:18, the Lord is longing to be gracious to us, He will rise to show compassion. We are the apple of His eye. He loves showing us favour, joy, peace, and love. Let us stir our faith up, believing, trusting, praying, and honouring God. Let's keep Him first in everything we do. Ecclesiastic asserts that there are different seasons in life. There is season of planting, weeding, and harvesting. All this season are important in different ways. If we can seek wisdom from God and use them wisely, we will harvest fruits at the right time, through Jesus Christ who strengthen us. After King David died, his son Solomon was depressed and exhausted, he was too young, surrounded by his father's enemy, and he did not know how to judge Gods people and to rule them. He had a dream, the lord came and asked him what he would like Him to do for him. He answered, give your servant an understanding mind and a hearing heart to judge your people that I may discern between good and bad. For who can Judge and rule your great people?

God answered him, because you have not asked for long life, riches nor your enemies lives, but you have asked for yourself understanding to recognise what is just and right, behold, I have done as you asked. I have given you a wise, discerning mind, so that no one before you was your equal, nor shall any arise after you equal to you. I have also given you what you have not asked, both riches and honour. So, there shall not be any among the Kings equal to you all the days of your life and if you will go My Way and keep My Statutes and My Commandments as your father David did, then I will lengthen your days. So here we can see God can give wisdom, understanding, discerning mind, long life, honour, wealthy and riches. This are all the things we desire but we can find them in the presence of God. And all what He need for us is to walk according to His Way, keeping His Statutes and His Commandments like King David, even He is promising long life. Help us Lord to walk according to your will. Give us a desire to seek you and to honour you and to leave according to your promises because they are Yes and Amen.

THE FATHER'S HEART

There was also a man of God who was called Elisha, who walked with God and trusted Him in every corner of his life. There was a Shunamite woman who catered for him every time he visited the area and the man of God thought she needed a reward. The woman had no child and her husband was old, Elisha prophesied to her, in 11 kings 4:16, ''at this season when the time comes around, you shall embrace a son.'' The woman conceived and bore a son at that season following year, according to the man of God prophesy. Later the child died, and the man of God raised him from dead. This is a lesson to learn that if we trust in God and walk according to his will, there is hope even in places where there is no hope. The woman had no child, God provided, the child died, God raised him. What a mighty God we serve.

Naaman was a commander of the army of the king of Syria, he was a great man with his master's acceptance because by him the lord had given him victory to Syria. He was also a mighty man of courage, but he was a leper. There was his wife's maid, who was a captive from Israel, she advised her mistress that there was a prophet in Israel who would heal the leprosy of her husband. Naaman Obeyed and went to meet the man of God in Israel. When Naaman arrived in Samaria, the man of God, Elisha told him to go and immerse himself into Jordan river seven times, and his skin shall be restored, and he shall be clean. After some doubt and persuasion from his servant, he obeyed. After immersing himself in the Jordan river seven times, his flesh was restored like that of a little child and he was clean. He returned to the man of God and said, now I know that there is no God in all the earth but in Israel. This is our true God, the creator of heaven and earth, He can do exceedingly, abundantly, and beyond what we can imagine. All what we need is trust and obey, for there is no other way to be happy in Him but to trust and obey.

There was also another day when the sons of the prophet borrowed the axe to cut the tree to build. While they were cutting the axe-head fell into the water. They reported to Elisha, and he asked where did it fell? Elisha cut off a stick and threw it in the river and the iron floated, and he picked it up. Another miracle from God He can float even the heavy metal like a balloon, 11 Kings 6: 1-7. We need to worship; He is worthy of our praise. Our redeemer, our deliverer, and our saviour, there is no other God like Him.

On another occasion, the king of Syria was warring against Israel, after counselling with his servants, he said, in such and such a place shall be my camp. Then Elisha sent to the king of Israel, saying, be aware for the Syrians are coming down there. Then the King of Israel sent to the place of which Elisha told and warned him, and thus he protected and saved himself repeatedly. And therefore, the mind of the King of Syria was greatly troubled by this thing. He called a meeting and wanted to know who among them takes his message to the King of Israel. One of the servants told him that it is Elisha the prophet who is in Israel, who tells the king of Israel the words that he speaks even in his bed chamber. After enquiring he was told that he lives in Dothan. So, the king of Assyria sent horses, chariots, and a great army and they surrounded the city. When Elisha servant rose early and went out, behold, an army was surrounding the City. He told Elisha, what shall we do? According to 11 kings 6:16, Elisha answered, fear not, for those with us are more than those with them. In verse 17 of the same chapter, Elisha prayed, Lord, I pray you open his eyes that he may see. And the Lord opened his eyes and he saw, and behold, the mountain was full of horses and chariots of fire round about Elisha. And when the Syrians came down to him, Elisha prayed to the Lord, smite this people with blindness. And God smote them with blindness. Then Elisha told the Syrian, this is not the way or the city. Follow me, and I will bring you to the man whom you are seeking. He lends them to Samaria, and he prayed again for their eyes to be opened and to their surprise they saw that they were amid Samaria, 11Kings6:8-24.

Then the king of Israel asked Elisha, shall I slay them? But Elisha answered, you shall not slay them, would you slay those you have taken captive with your sword and bow? Set bread and water before them that they may eat and drink and return to their master. The king prepared great provision for them, and when they had eaten and drunk, he sent them away and they went to their master. The bands of Syria came no more into the land of Israel. This message teaches us that if we walk closer with God, he can open our ears to hear what our enemies are planning, even at a distance, it can be through vision, dream or a small voice behind us. We are also surrounded by horses and chariots of fire, which the army of the living God, to protect us from our enemies. There is also power of prayers, Elisha said smite this people with blindness, and God smote them with blindness. Then he misdirected them to Samaria.

Similarly, another miraculous power happened in Samaria which can also show us the power of God when we walk and trust Him and also the fruit of rejecting Him and choosing our ways, the son of Jezebel was the King by the time and they had sinned against God by worshiping idols and his father Ahab had taken the land of Naboth which was inherited land by force. So, the Lord let the Syrian to besiege Samaria, King Ben-hadad gathered his whole army and besieged Samaria. As a result, a great famine broke out, which led to a donkey's head to be sold for eighty shekels of silver and a fourth of a cab of dove's dung to be sold for five shekels of silver. This shaws how desperate they were because according to Jews law, they were not around to eat donkey or any animal with no split hooves. But here we can see they were desperate to get one. That is the outcome of separating ourselves from God and searching our own way. It might feel comfortable at the beginning, but it is a gold coated outside but inside is more painful than imagined.

As the king of Israel was passing by the wall, a woman cried to him, help my lord, o king! No, let the Lord help you! From where I can get you help! Out of the threshing flour, or wine press? She answered, this woman said to me, give me your son we may eat him today and we will eat mine tomorrow. So, we boiled my son and ate him. The next day, I said to her, give your son so we may eat him, but she had hidden her son. When the king heard this, he rent his clothes. And as he went on upon the wall, the people looked and behold, he wore sack clothes inside. Then he said may God do so to me, and more also, if Elisha son of Shaphat shall stand on Him this day. It is very easy and comfortable to blame those who are around us, but it does not solve the problem. It is very hard to accept our mistake and to learn from them. The God and the prophet, whom he was angry and bitter with, are the only hope he had. So, it was easier to say forgive Lord, for I have sinned against you and against your people and see the cry of your people.

THE FATHER'S HEART

While Elisha sat in his house with the elders. The King sent a man ahead of him to behead Elisha, but before the massager arrived, Elisha told the elders, see how the son of Jezebel a murderer is sending a man to remove my head. Look, when the messenger arrive, shut the door, and hold it fast against him. Is not the sound of his master's feet just behind him? And the messenger arrived together with the king. The king said, this evil is from God, why should we wait any longer expecting Him to withdraw His punishment? Elisha, what can we done now? Elisha said, hear the word of the lord. Tomorrow about this time a measure of fine flour will sell for a shekel and two measure of barley for a shekel in the gate of Samaria. But one of the captains on whose hand the king leaned answered the man of God and said, if the windows in heaven open could this thing be? But Elisha said, you shall see it with your own eyes, but you shall not eat it.

By the entrance of the city's gate there were four lepers. They said to each other, if we go to the city we will die of hunger, let go over to the army of the Syrians, if they spare us alive, we shall live, and if they kill us, we shall die. They arose in the twilight and went to the Syrian camp; no man was there. For the Lord had made the Syrian army hear a noise of great army. They had said to one another, the king of Israel has hired the Hittite and Egyptian kings to come upon us. So, the Syrians arose and fled in the twilight and left their tents, horses, donkeys, left the camp as it was, and fled for their lives. When the lepers came to the edge of the camp, they went into the tent and ate and drunk and carried away silver, gold, and clothing, and hid them in the darkness. They entered anther tent and carried from there also and hide as well.

Then they said to one another, we are not doing right. This is the day of good news and we are silent and do not speak up. If we wait until day light, some punishment will come upon us. Let us go and tell the king household, that there is no sound of man, only horses, donkeys tied and tents as they were. One of the king's servant said, let us send some men with the remaining horses, if they are caught and killed they will be no worse off than all the multitude of Israel left in the city to be consumed. They came back with good report. All the way was strewing with clothing and equipment which the Syrians had cast away in their flight. The people went out and plundered the tents of the Syrians. And so, a measure of fine flour according to what the man of God Elisha had spoken was sold for a shekel, and two measure of barley for a shekel. But according to words spoken by Elisha, the king had chosen the captain who was leaning on him, to oversee the gate. The starving people trampled him in the gate as they were struggling to get through for food and he died. This is the man who said even if the windows of heaven open could such thing be. But

THE FATHER'S HEART

Elisha had told him, you will see but you will not eat 11 Kings 7:19-20. This confirm the way the bible says, to God one day is like a thousand days and a thousand days like a day. Everything was turned around with a twinkling of an eye. The food was plenty, and freedom sustained when the King went to seek God through the man of God.

NOTES